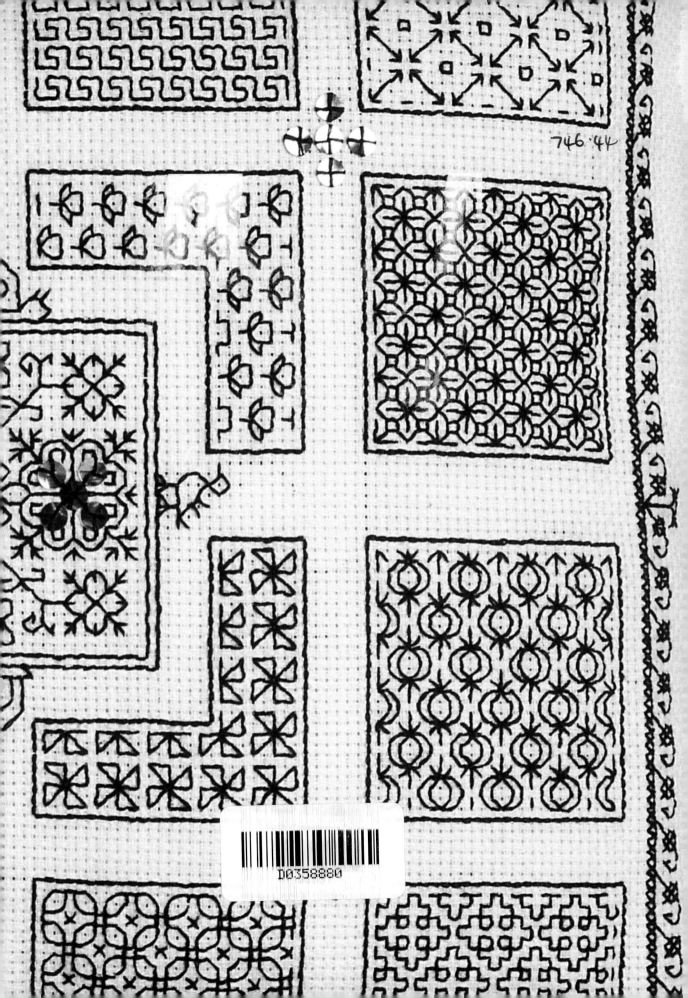

746·44

D0358880

THIS IS THE PROPERTY OF
SOUTH WORCESTERSHIRE COLLEGE
SCHOOL OF ARTS

£6.00

Needlecraft Magazine's

COMPLETE GUIDE TO
Blackwork

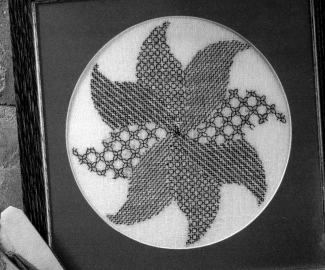

Needlecraft Magazine's

COMPLETE GUIDE TO
Blackwork

Amanda Cox
with Barbara Phillips

Future
BOOKS

Dedication

To my three daughters, Elisabeth, Sophie and Alice,
without whom the passage of this book would have
been so much easier

First published in 1995 by
Future Books
A division of Future Publishing Limited
30 Monmouth Street, Bath BA1 2BW

Blackwork design copyright © Barbara Phillips 1995
Text and photographs copyright © Future Publishing 1995

The moral right of the author has been asserted

Designed by Harriet Athay
Text by Amanda Cox
Pattern designs by Barbara Phillips
Edited by Kate John
Photography by Jonathan Fisher

All rights reserved. No part of this publication may be reproduced,
stored in a retrieval system or transmitted in any form or by any means, electronic, mechani-
cal or otherwise, without the prior written permission of the copyright owner.

A CIP catalogue record of this book is
available from the British Library

ISBN: 1 85981 090 X

Reprographics by Quadcolour Ltd., Warley, West Midlands
Printed and bound by BPC Paulton Books Ltd.
A member of the British Printing Company
2 4 6 8 10 9 7 5 3 1

We take great care to ensure that what we print is accurate, but we cannot accept liability for
any mistakes or misprints.

If you would like more information on our other stitching titles please write to:
The Publisher, Future Books
at the above address

Contents

INTRODUCTION & HISTORY

Blackwork designs and techniques have been passed down through the ages.

Welcome to *Needlecraft* magazine's *Complete Guide to Blackwork*. Along with the ground swell of interest in many forms of needlecraft, blackwork has undergone a steady revival in recent times. Blackwork is '...the technique of stitching counted thread embroidery patterns in black threads on white fabric.' A rather lacklustre definition that does not do justice to a technique that has an intriguing past and can offer plenty to the modern stitching enthusiast.

Needlecraft magazine's *Complete Guide to Blackwork* aims to place blackwork in its historical context, whilst explaining its easy-to-follow design techniques. To inspire you to further heights, we look at how to design your own blackwork, which will prove that inspiration is easy to find, even in the most unlikely places. To help the design process, there are over 80 blackwork clearly charted patterns in the pattern library. A superb collection of original blackwork designs created by our own Barbara Phillips is beautifully photographed, clearly charted and complete with step by step instructions. For the more experienced needlewoman, Needlecraft magazine's 'Complete Guide to Blackwork' will be an invaluable source book you will refer to again and again. If you have never considered exploring this exciting embroidery technique, this book will open your eyes to its unique potential.

Historical background

Blackwork embroidery is enjoying a well-deserved revival today which mirrors its popularity in Tudor times. By looking at its historical background, we can begin to appreciate its pedigree. Despite its beginnings so long ago, it has a freshness and contemporary feel that makes it an exciting technique for today's fabrics and threads. In England, blackwork became very fashionable during the reign of Henry VIII and continued to gain popularity during the sixteenth century, with interest waning again sometime around 1630.

However, the origins of this style of counted thread embroidery are diverse and ancient. Geometric repeated patterns have long been used for decorative purposes, appearing on mosaics, floor tiles and brickwork in the time of the Romans, the ancient Greeks and other ancient civilisations. Examples of the technique have also been found in many European countries and is seen to this day in the traditional peasant embroidery of the Slavonic countries.

To understand the rise in popularity of blackwork in Europe throughout the 15th Century and 16th Century, we need to take a look at the influences from further afield,

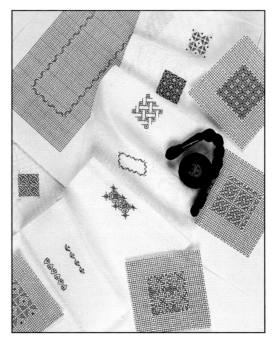

in particular from the Moorish civilisation of North Africa. The Moors had ruled in Spain for over eight hundred years; finally being overthrown in 1492 by King Ferdinand and Queen Isabella. After such an extended period of time, the influences from the Islamic culture of the Moors on Spanish society and culture were considerable. The areas of textile crafts, carpet-making and embroidery particularly reflect the Islamic principles of symmetry in design. Elements of early Tudor blackwork are more geometric in design, reflecting this influence.

That being so, however, there is mention of the blackwork technique in England before the time of the Tudors: the *Canterbury Tales* were written at the end of the fourteenth century, which predates the Tudors by two hundred years. In the *Carpenter's Tale*, Geoffrey Chaucer describes the blackwork detail on the costume of the carpenter's wife:-

'*...Her smock was white, embroidery repeated*
Its pattern on the collar front and back,
Inside and out, it was of silk and black.
And all the ribbons of her milky mutch*
Were made to match her collar, and such...' **1**

* A linen or muslin cap worn by women of the period.

The closely textured stitching was on the visible areas of the undershirt which was worn by men and women alike under their outer garments. Subject to much hard wear and tear, the blackwork served to strengthen the fabric. This was one of the practical uses for blackwork which continued into the time of Henry VIII and beyond.

So we can see that blackwork was in evidence before Tudor times, but the immense rise in popularity during the 1600s was due to the presence of Catherine of Aragon, the daughter of Ferdinand and Isabella, who arrived from Spain in 1501. Originally married to Arthur, the elder son of Henry VII, Catherine brought with her a great love for this counted thread technique, which through her enthusiasm, became known as 'Spanish Work' and it is in the early period of her influence that we see the echoes of the Moorish influence. Arthur died a year after the marriage and as it was unconsummated, Catherine was married again, this time to Arthur's younger brother Henry: thus she became the first of Henry VIII's infamous 'Six Wives'. It is well documented that Henry's reign was tempestuous and eventful, but it is also important to note that Catherine was Queen of England for over twenty-five years. During this long period of time, she held sway over the Court. Her passion for 'Spanish Work' fired the enthusiasm of the English courtiers and the technique became firmly established. It remained in vogue for over one hundred and twenty-five years. During this time, the term 'Spanish Work' was eventually replaced by 'blackwork' as Spain and all things Spanish fell out of favour, when Henry divorced Catherine in 1534.

The demand for fabrics was great as the fashion for blackwork grew to encompass bedlinen and household textiles like wall-hangings, towels and the like. Home-produced linen or a linen and cotton mix called fustian for the poorer classes were the traditional choices for these items. However, for their needs, the wealthy imported finer fabrics whose names belie their origins: 'holland' cloth, cambric and lawn from Cambrai and Laon in France.

There are fine examples of blackwork embroidery featured in portraits of the time, but unfortunately there are not too many pieces of embroidered fabric that have remained. Blackwork was sometimes used as a disguise for dirt in an age not known for

1 The Canterbury Tales, translated by Nevill Coghill (Penguin)

its hygiene practices! Undergarments and other fabrics used in the home were occasionally and imperfectly washed, but the sumptuous outer garments sadly were not. The manufacture of soaps was also a crude and imperfect art at the time, with ingredients which probably contributed to the disintegration of much fabric of the period.

For those who could not afford the costly black embroidery silk imported from Holland, home-dyeing was the only alternative. The mixture of lye, elder bark, crushed walnut shells and sulphuric acid in the dye was a corrosive mixture that was not even colour-fast. The oils and grime of accumulated wear, as well as the potency of the dye used in cheap embroidery threads caused the fibres of the threads to rot. Where costume has survived, often the only proof of blackwork embroidery is the evidence of holes or blank areas on the fabric.

Despite the lack of surviving costume, we are fortunate to have many fine examples of blackwork embroidery in portraits of the time. The double running stitch favoured in the technique is also known as Holbein Stitch after Hans Holbein, the sixteenth century Court painter. Having gained the patronage of King Henry VIII in 1536, he painted the portraits of many aristocrats dressed in the fashions of the day. It is from these representations that we see excellent examples of rich blackwork embroidery. Many court painters of the time have left us with a fascinating legacy of the costume of the time.

After the symmetry of the initial Spanish influences, blackwork design evolved and favoured a freer interpretation; outlined shapes such as fruit and flowers were filled with geometric patterns. These featured largely on bedlinen and other household articles, as well as sleeves, collars and cuffs. Metallic thread was used to decorate and enliven the black on white embroidery; this was known as 'silver-gilt'. The manufacturing technique involved extruding gold-coated

silver wire very finely. These strands were then flattened and wrapped around silk thread or left plain and stitched as a metallic wire. For the lower classes, the delicacy of blackwork stitching provided an alternative to costly lace, which was taxed in the Tudor and early Jacobean times. A Royal Court Edict prohibited the wearing of lace by any other than the higher ranks of the nobility. Consequently, the addition of blackwork suggested the trappings of aristocracy to the aspiring upwardly mobile.

As sophistication in textile developments introduced more coloured threads and greater versatility, blackwork was perceived as rather dull and interest gradually waned over the next few centuries. In this century, during the 1920s and 1930s, blackwork was briefly revived in a way that reflected the traditional methods of outlined forms filled with patterning. The modern interest in the subject began in the 1960s, but the trend in design is towards the blend of tone and texture rather than the strict forms of the Tudor style of embroidery.

Black and white is a classic combination which has become part of the modern design ethos. It is remarkable to consider that a technique which was fashionable over four hundred years ago has spanned the centuries so effortlessly by embodying this ethos. Today, the versatility of blackwork is enjoyed by a growing number of people who appreciate its simplicity and wide application. With just a few embroidery stitches, a world of creativity is accessible to everyone. We are fortunate to be able to choose from a great variety of natural and synthetic threads to create a style of embroidery which has strong echoes of its rich past but with modern interpretation. Blackwork is definitely here to stay and will continue to evolve as long as it is practised. Enjoy our collection of projects and pattern library and be inspired to discover the hidden secrets of blackwork for yourself.

PATTERN & DESIGN

A traditional stitching technique that is highly versatile in its application.

Density and Tone

Every blackwork pattern has a unique tonal quality and the careful juxtaposition of light and dark patterns will add texture and impact to your designs. The modern interpretation of blackwork favours this approach rather than the more formalised technique of outlining each pattern, which can be more limited in application. By using the patterns as blocks of tone, you can introduce subtle shading effects which add pace and a three-dimensional sense to your designs. This tonality can be achieved in the following ways:

The following points refer to the Sampler project on page 57.

• The denser the pattern of lines, the darker the tone of the finished piece. A pattern with few lines over a wide area adds space and light to your design. Take one simple shape and add lines to build up the density of the pattern.(1)

• By careful selection of fine and thick threads, shaded effects can be introduced. The same pattern stitched in flower thread and then in Coton perlé No. 5 has a completely different look. Try using two types of thread within one pattern repeat to add dimension to your work. (2)

By considering these two aspects when deciding on patterns, your number of choices is expanded to a staggering degree. Doodling and drawing patterns out on squared paper is an excellent way of crystallising your ideas: when you see the lines on the paper, the design really starts to take shape. Always stitch a practice piece on a scrap of fabric before committing it to 'the real thing'.

Changing the scale

The number of patterns for use in blackwork embroidery is limitless: the geometric qualities of the patterns means that any example can be modified in terms of scale. By changing the number of threads over which a motif is stitched, a completely different effect is created. This in turn will affect the tonal quality of the pattern: it is an interesting exercise to see how many variations the same pattern can reveal when modified in this way. If you stitch the same pattern over two threads and then over four threads, the depth of tone moves from darker to light. (3) Add to this the use of different weights of thread, as seen above and the potential variety of pattern is staggering.

Our library of patterns are charted on a squared grid for clarity, and can be stitched

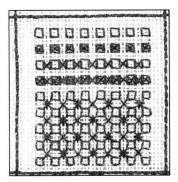

Square F on Sampler

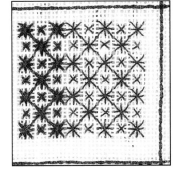

Square K on Sampler

Square B on Sampler

as seen, but they are not set in stone! Get out your squared paper and pencil again to try out some of the modifications listed here.

Tips on choosing patterns

Faced with an infinite choice of pattern permutation, where do you start?

• The choice of pattern should allow for sufficient pattern repeats within the specified design area. This will allow for the full effect of the pattern to be realised. A large area needs a bold pattern, whereas a smaller area requires a more compact repeat.
• A pattern within an outlined area should always follow the angle of the design shape. For a shape on the diagonal, choose a pattern which can follow that diagonal line. This will produce a more harmonious, integrated effect.
• Sometimes you will be unable to stitch a whole motif because it is interrupted by the outline of your chosen shape. Always stitch the partial pattern following the lines of the completed motif. This might mean that you have to split a thread in the fabric weave, but the most important thing is that the direction of the patterning is not changed.
• How do you want to use shading and tone in your design? Is it to create a 3D effect or to introduce texture and density to something more abstract?

Reversible Blackwork

Where both sides of the work is visible, you can work blackwork motifs so that they are reversible. The process of stitching is more complicated as the lines have to be continuous on both sides of the work.

Borders

Borders add a decorative flourish to your work. Quite often, elements of a filling pattern can be taken on their own to produce a fine border. Some forward planning is required when turning the corners of borders to achieve a neat finish.

1 Take a frameless mirror and place it at an angle of 45° on the border.

2 You will need to move it along the row until the pattern makes a suitable corner. You might need to modify the pattern lines a little to make it work.

3 Some border repeats have an even number of stitches, and others odd, so careful thought is needed to ensure that the chosen border fits symmetrically around the central stitching.

Use of different stitches

Blackwork and backstitch are natural partners: the beauty of this technique is that such distinctive effects can be created with a few simple stitches. These are backstitch, running backstitch and double running stitch. Other decorative stitches most commonly used are double cross stitch, also called Smyrna stitch which produces a star-like effect and Algerian eyelet stitch in which all the points of the star are stitched through the same centre hole, pulling the threads to produce a tiny hole.

Blackwork patterns as filling

Another way to use blackwork embroidery patterns is as a decorative infill within free shape motifs. This can be seen clearly in the examples of English costume of the sixteenth century, where fruits, leaves and other motifs were filled with patterning. Our popular 'Blackwork Ladies' are good examples of this technique. Outlining is always added after the shapes have been in-filled. There is a choice of several stitch options for outlining. It is interesting to see how the emphasis changes with the strength of outlining. For a subtle outline, choose *plain* or overcast *backstitch*; for more definition *stem stitch*, *chain stitch* or *couching* can be used to great effect. Don't forget that different threads can add more weight to an outline if you wish.

DESIGN YOUR OWN BLACKWORK PATTERN

An exciting way to explore the full potential of the Blackwork style.

Introduction

You Will Need

- **Photograph or sketch**
- **Transparent graph paper or tracing paper and squared paper**
- **Pencil and eraser**

As you can see from the variety of dazzling projects in this book, the versatility of blackwork knows no bounds. Feel inspired to create something for yourself and don't know how to do it or where to start? Well, look no further - believe it or not, there is inspiration all around, even in the most mundane objects and unlikely settings. Heightening your awareness of the potential of surroundings will mean that you are never short of inspiration again.

One of the most abundant design sources which is readily accessible is wrought iron. Just take a look in your locality: gates and railings in parks, gardens and churchyards for a start. Once you have begun to look for ideas, you will be surprised at just how much wrought ironwork there is out there! Its intricate curls and repeated patterning makes it an ideal source for adaptation on to fabric.

In the following 'case studies', you will see the evolution of the design process. These simple examples were not difficult to find, in fact once you start looking for possible inspiration, you will notice it everywhere! Follow the step by step instructions below and you can't go wrong.

How to start

1 The aim is to translate the image you have obtained in a photograph, a sketch, postcard etc. on to squared paper as a chart for stitching on to fabric. If the image is not the size you require for your design, enlarge or reduce it using a photocopier.

2 Draw your chosen pattern onto transparent graph paper by laying the sheet over the photocopy or photograph. Remember that you will have to modify the pattern first to suit the constraints of squared paper and evenweave fabric (this means no curved lines!). If there are parts of the original outline that don't work well, don't be afraid to modify them or even leave them out. This is where you can be flexible - use your source as a starting point; don't let it limit your creativity.

NOTE: If you don't have transparent graph paper, do this in three stages
i) Transfer the design to ordinary tracing paper.
ii) Place a piece of graph paper over the tracing paper and stick the two pieces of paper to a window. This allows you to see through the graph paper to the tracing beneath.
iii) Trace off the design to fit within the grid of squares.

This is your blackwork pattern in its raw state. By adding or taking away elements you can then adapt it to its final form.

You can experiment with the pattern to produce different results:
• by rotating the pattern 45° or 90°, the form of the pattern changes. Some patterns are completely symmetrical and do not change, others take on a different look altogether.
• adapting or extracting specific elements within a pattern. Sometimes a section of a pattern can be used as a border in its own

Gate example

Props for photoshoot: *Polaroid photo of gate; graph paper; tracing paper; 28HPI evenweave; black flower thread.*

This design is taken from an intricately wrought iron gate, spotted on a Sunday afternoon walk. Although the photograph wasn't too clear, I was able to see enough detail to transfer the pattern straight to squared paper. I experimented with the positioning of the patterns:
- A - by mirroring each repeat, I reproduced the design on the gate.
- B - in a vertical repeat sequence, the pattern creates a different effect.
- C - by taking one element which looked promising, in this case, one half of the design, two attractive borders emerged.

The choice of design can originate from an ornate object. Architectural designs are especially popular.

A

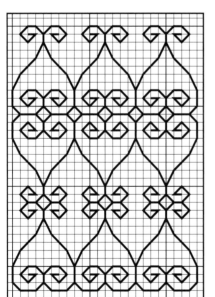

B

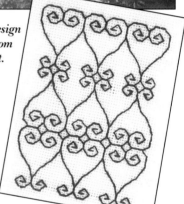

C

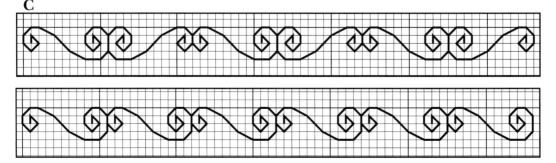

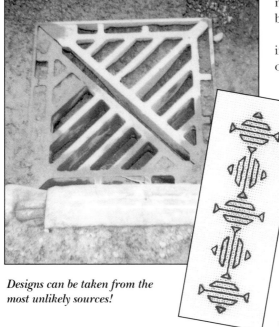

Designs can be taken from the most unlikely sources!

nately rotating the motif, the final effect is bold and very modern.

If it rains, don't despair - you can find inspiration without setting foot outside your own home! Wall tiles, furniture and textiles are rich sources of design to fire your imagination.

These simple examples show just how simple it can be to create something that is truly yours. You might not feel that you are 'artistic', but the beauty of blackwork means that anyone who can draw a straight line can design a geometric motif! By exploring the qualities of simple patterns, you will discover the hidden secrets of blackwork for yourself. Creativity is like any skill - it needs to be practised. Start to keep a scrapbook of photos and sketches, locations of potential design sources which you can build up over time. Keeping your eyes open for design possibilities is a productive and absorbing use of your time - but take care, it can become addictive!

Drain cover

Props for photoshoot: *Polaroid photo of drain cover; graph paper; tracing paper; 28HPI even-weave; black flower thread.*

Mundane in the extreme, you might say, but the potential of this muddy drain cover caught my eye because of its wonderful straight lines and geometric form. When the shape was transferred to squared paper, I felt that it needed some adaptation to work on the fabric. In the event, the final pattern was a simplified version of the original. You might feel that your pattern needs something added to it rather than taken away - don't be afraid to experiment and change your mind. Stitching the pattern on a scrap of fabric to see the final effect is always helpful. Save these practice pieces to put in your scrapbook.

The geometric lines of this pattern lends itself very well to a border repeat. By alter-

Pattern Darning

Pattern darning is another counted thread embroidery technique that can be incorporated into blackwork. It adds intensity as the stitching is often done in geometric block patterns. The placing of patterns on the fabric is paramount as the effects are created by the spaces left in between the blocks of stitching as much as the stitching itself.

Pattern darning requires nothing more than simple running stitch in straight lines to achieve superb decorative results. For this reason, it is a good starting point for beginners. Use a combination of vertical, horizontal and diagonal lines of running stitch to produce an incredible variety of patterned effects.

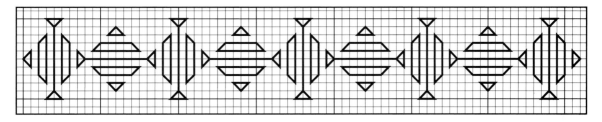

The final result of pattern darning is reversible, which makes it a practical choice for curtain and towel borders. Its simplicity lends itself to children's clothes and other items which require a homespun finish.

Double darning is a variant of pattern darning, in which blocks of colour are created by completely covering the fabric with lines of stitching.

Materials for pattern darning

You can use any evenweave fabric for pattern darning: the pattern will grow much more quickly on a coarser weave fabric. Fine weaves will need more lines of stitching to build up a pattern.

Threads

The guidelines for blackwork apply here: the weight of the thread and fabric should be more or less the same. Different threads give a different effect: for a firm line, choose a thread that can be worked in a single strand like coton perlé or broder Spécial. For good coverage of the fabric weave, as in double darning, choose stranded cotton.

How to position patterns

To help you position patterns as part of a more complex design, follow this method. Referring to your tacking line, start stitching from the centre, at the top of the pattern. Don't pull the thread right through to start; leave a generous length at your starting point. Work to the left hand edge of the stitching area in running stitch, ensuring that you follow your chart to get the correct spacing of the stitches. When the left edge is reached, stitch back to the centre point following the chart. At the centre, thread the needle with the other end of thread you have left and stitch on to the right hand side. This line can then be used as a reference as you build up the patterns.

How to start

1 Pattern darning is usually worked with the fabric held in the hand, but you can use an embroidery hoop if you prefer.

2 Work lines of tacking stitches across and down the centre of the fabric and then mark corresponding pencil lines on your chart. This will help you to keep your place as you stitch. Remove the tacking threads when the design is completed.

3 To secure the thread, start each line of pattern with a back stitch.

Work a simple running stitch, counting the number of threads between each stitch to create the patterns.

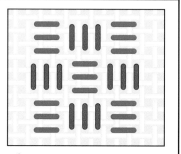

4 Pattern darning can be worked in any direction, from left to right or right to left.

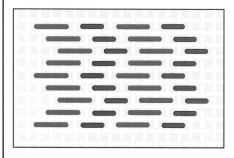

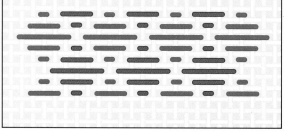

TECHNICAL INFORMATION

Materials and methods used, including tips on how to assemble your work.

Fabrics

As blackwork is a counted thread embroi dery technique, it is worked on even-weave fabrics, traditionally cotton or linen. Today we are fortunate to have a wider choice of fabrics than the Tudors. These range from the heavy canvasses through to fine silk gauzes. All these are suitable for blackwork embroidery. The rule of thumb when choosing the right thread for the fabric is that the thickness of the thread should correspond to the weight of the evenweave.

A prime consideration when choosing a fabric is a regularity in the weave of the fabric; this will avoid random distortion to the geometric qualities of the patterns. There is no reason why you could not experiment on aida or any other fabric which is woven in an evenweave style. Why not stitch samples using dress or furnishing fabric remnants with an evenweave to see what effects you can create?

Most of our projects are stitched on 28 or 30HPI count fabrics. If you are unfamiliar with the abbreviation: HPI stands for holes per inch of fabric. The more holes per inch, the smaller the stitches. The different threads used in the projects vary in thickness, but nothing is used that distorts the weave of the fabric. Any thread can be used, but when the desired effect is crisp and distinct, it is best to avoid woollen yarns which give a 'fuzzy' look.

Types of thread

We have used DMC threads for all our projects: as the predominant colour used is black which requires no accurate colour-matching, there is no problem when using threads from other thread manufacturers. Where other colours are incorporated, the conversion numbers are approximate.

The use of colour in blackwork is a modern evolution of the technique, adding tone and texture to the stitching. It is used with great effect in our projects, and lends a truly contemporary feel to a design. Choose your fabric carefully when you stitch in colour: you must ensure a good contrast between the colour of the fabric and the thread for maximum impact. For example, a rich brown on beige looks stunning; dark blue on a paler shade of blue is cool and stylish.

The threads stitched in the photograph will give you an idea of the variety of threads that can be used in blackwork: some of these threads may be unfamiliar to you, but they are all available from good needlecraft stockists.

A - Polyester sewing thread

Ordinary sewing thread can add a beautifully delicate touch to your blackwork: when juxtaposed with a thicker thread the effect is dramatic. Choose a good quality polyester thread which will give a much smoother, more distinct line than a cotton thread.

B - 1 strand stranded cotton

Stranded cotton is a very versatile thread: it comes in six divisble strands and any number of them can be combined to add contrasts of texture and tone to a wide variety of fabrics. It is a silky textured thread and comes in a range of around 400 colours as well as black! One strand gives a delicate effect, well suited to finer fabrics, but works equally well as a contrast on heavier fabrics.

C - Flower thread

This is used in one strand, Flower thread has a matt finish and a subtle soft texture, which is highly suited to blackwork as well as other types of embroidery.

If you are not using a mount then cut the wadding to the size of the lacing board. Place the piece of wadding centrally on the board.

3 Centre your fabric over the wadding and lacing board either by eye or by measuring carefully. Push pins through the fabric and into the board along the top edge. Use the holes of the fabric as a guide to ensure that you are pinning it straight. If you prefer, centre the fabric over the lacing board and then using a ruler and set square, draw lines on the fabric at the edges of the lacing board. Follow these lines when you are pinning the fabric to the board and this will keep it straight.

4 Pull the fabric gently and pin along the bottom in the same way. Repeat this process along the sides, again being careful to keep the fabric straight.

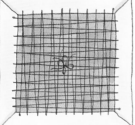

5 Working from the back of the project, thread a large-eyed needle with a thick strong cotton like crochet cotton and tie a knot at the end. Lace from top to bottom using an 'under-and-over' motion. Stop half way across the back and repeat from the other side. When you reach the centre, go back and remove the slack from the threads one by one before knotting the two ends.

6 Repeat this process across the two other edges. If you run out of thread before you reach the centre, join in a new piece with a reef knot.

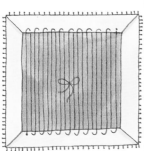

7 Fold in the corners, stitch in place and remove the pins. Your work is now ready to put into your frame. Glass will protect your work from fading and dust although you won't be able to see the stitching as clearly.

How to mount your work into a card

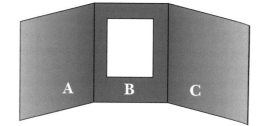

1 Place your stitched fabric right side up and place the opening of the card centrally over it. Push pins through the fabric at the top, bottom and sides of the opening. If you place your fabric on a cork placemat or even the carpet then the pins will stay in place. Take the card gently off the fabric so as not to disturb the pins.

2 Place a few strips of double sided tape or spread a small amount of glue on to the inside of the card at B round all the edges. Place the card back onto the fabric over the pins and stick down. The positioning pins will act as guides so that the card is placed centrally first time.

3 Turn the card over to the wrong side with the bottom of the design towards you. Place strips of double sided tape or spread some glue round the edges of the inside of the card at A. If you are using wadding then cut a piece to the same size as the card opening then place it over the fabric where the opening of the card is. Press A firmly down onto B.

4 If you are using glue then keep a dry cloth handy to remove any excess. Place the finished card under a heavy weight to ensure that it sticks firmly. If you have used tape then this won't be necessary.

STITCH GUIDES

Illustrated instructions, designed to assist your stitching techniques.

Keep each step of the stitches separate to keep the tension in the fabric even. This means taking the needle down through the fabric and pulling the thread right through and then bringing the needle up again and pulling through in the same way.

Back stitch

Bring the needle up at 1, down at 2, up at 3 and so on following the line on the chart and working over the number of threads specified each time.

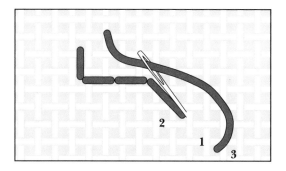

Double Running or Holbein stitch

This is a running stitch worked in two runs. Make a line of running stitch. Return along the same stitching line in running stitch, filling in the gaps left in the first run. You will need to turn your work 180° for the return run.

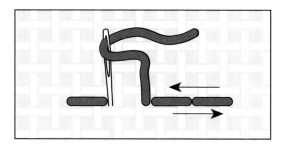

Running Backstitch

This stitch is a combination of running stitch and backstitch. Make the first stitch a running stitch - up at 1 and down at 2 - and the second a backstitch - up at 3, down at 4. Repeat this sequence of alternating the two stitches to complete the desired pattern.

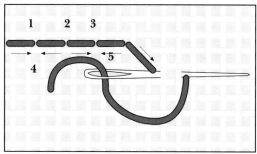

Cross stitch

(A) To make one cross stitch, bring the needle up at 1, down at 2, up at 3 and down at 4.
(B) To work horizontal rows, stitch all the way across the work diagonal stitches back over them to form the cross stitches by following the numbers.

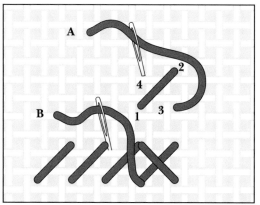

French knots

Bring the needle up where you want the knot to be. Hold the thread as it comes out of the fabric and place the needle behind it.
Twist the thread around the needle - the more times you wind it, the larger the knot will be. Two twists are adequate for most knots.
Keeping the thread taut so the loops are tight round the needle, push the needle

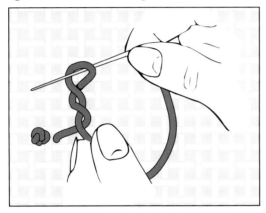

down in the fabric at the point where it first emerged.
Hold the thread taut until the needle passes all the way fabric. Pull gently, but firmly, to form a knot. Repeat as necessary.

Long stitch

Bring the needle up at 1, down at 2, up at 3, and down at 4. Follow the chart for the exact placement of the stitch.

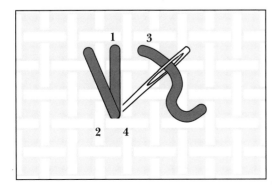

Algerian Eyelet stitch

Begin from top right and work into the centre each time. Bring the needle up at 1, down into the centre A, up at 2, down into the centre A, up at 3 and so on. Continue to work in a clockwise direction until all the points are completed.

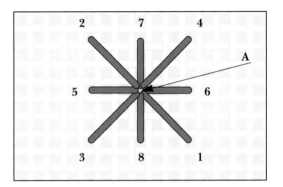

Double Cross stitch or Smyrna stitch

This stitch has a star-like effect. Come up at 1, go down at 2 and up at 3 just below 2. Go down again at 4, up at 5 in between 2 and 3 and down at 6. Come up at 7 between 2 and 4 and down at 8 to complete the stitch.

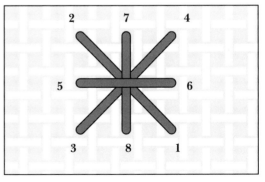

Overcast Backstitch

Having stitched a line of backstitch, make the line more intense by weaving the thread under and over each stitch in the row. This technique is completed on the surface of the fabric.

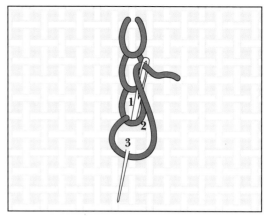

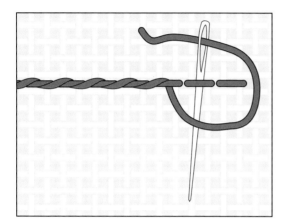

Couching

Using the line on the chart as a your guide, bring up the thread to be couched at the starting point of the line as indicated. Place small stitches equally spaced, over the laid thread to secure it to the fabric.

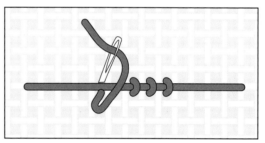

Stem stitch

Bring the needle up just below the stitching line at 1, down at 2 just below the line and back up at 3. Continue along the line, always working back on yourself. Keep the stitches small and of equal length

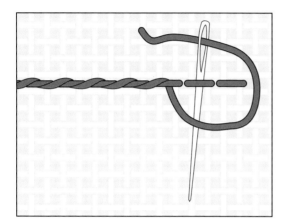

Satin stitch

Work a series of straight stitches close together, carefully following the design line. Make sure that you keep the edges of the stitches as neat as possible to show the shape of the design clearly.

Chain stitch

Bring then needle up at 1. Insert it again at 2 and with the thread under the needle bring it out at 3. Repeat this keeping the stitches the same length. To finish off the stitching, make a small stitch over the last loop to secure the thread.(See top right.)

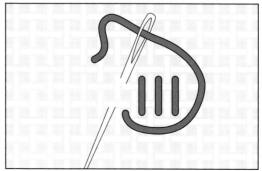

COMPLETE GUIDE TO
Blackwork
Placemat and Napkin

How to mitre your corners

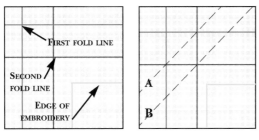

Diagram 1   **Diagram 2**

1 Find the middle point between the red line and the lines of drawn threads. Fold over at this point - and press it down, forming a crease. (See blue line on Diagram One). This is the finished hemline.

2 Using these lines to guide you, lightly draw a diagonal line A with a soft pencil and ruler (see Diagram Two). This is the outer fold line. Now draw the inner fold line B, parallel to line A.

3 Cut off the corner of the fabric along outer line A. Fold this edge along line B to make a crease. Turn the hem under at the cor-

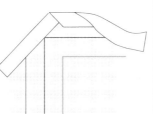

Diagram 3

ner enclosing this cut edge. Fold along the red line first to neaten the raw edge and then along the blue line so that the two edges of the fabric meet in a neat corner. (See Diagram Three). When it is folded on both sides, the edges of the mitred corner can be slipstitched together with a matching thread. (See Diagram Four)

4 Tack the folded mitred hem in place before either hemstitching or slipstitching it into place.

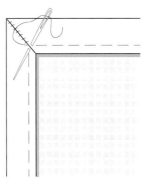

Diagram 4

Antique Hem Stitch Guide

1 Always work the hemstitching from the back of the fabric. The threads are stitched in groups of two. Secure your thread in the hem. Work all stitching through one thickness of fabric so that the vertical stitches will not show through on the right side.

2 Working from right to left, come up at 1, one thread below the drawn threads. Go down at 2 behind the drawn threads and up at 3, two threads further left.

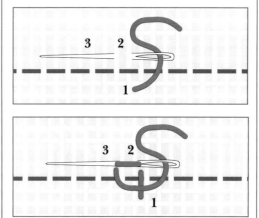

3 Now go down again at 2 and up again at 3 making a double stitch.

4 Insert the needle vertically down at 3 between the two layers of hem and up at 4, directly below 3 and in line with 1.

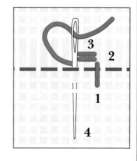

5 Repeat these steps across the fabric, ensuring that all the stitches are the same size. To finish off neatly, run the needle through the back of a few stitches.

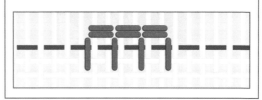

PETAL IN PATCHWORK

A striking combination of Blackwork stitches makes an unusual gift.

You Will Need

- 28 HPI evenweave - 11x11in(28x28cm), antique white (ref. NJ429.10)
- DMC stranded cotton - 310, black
- Tapestry needle - size 26
- Tacking thread
- Thin card - 6x6in (15x15cm), white
- Tissue paper
- Scissors
- Soft pencil and rubber
- Frame with coloured mounting card
- 2 oz. wadding

How to start

1 Transfer the petal outline from the template to a piece of card and cut it out.

2 Draw a 7in (18cm) square on a piece of graph paper. Mark the divisions in the square as shown in the diagram. Place a dot at the centre of the square.

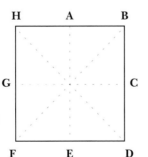

3 Match the dot on the template with the dot at the centre of the square. Place the template vertically on the line from the centre to point A.

4 Draw round the outside of the template. Moving clockwise, place the template at the next intersection of dots (point B), draw round it and then repeat the process right the way round the circle to point H.

5 Rub out the inside of the petals where they overlap, so that it looks as if they are lying on top of one another in a clockwise direction.

6 Now carefully trace the design onto tissue paper. Position the tissue paper on the evenweave fabric, making sure that the design is lined up with the grain of the fabric. (If not, your stitching will be distorted and the technique will not be successful).

7 Using small running stitches, carefully baste through both layers around all the drawn outlines. Now, tear way the tissue paper very gently and the tacked outlines will be left on the fabric.

How to stitch the design

1 Work each stitch over two threads of the evenweave fabric. The blackwork patterns are worked using one strand of black stranded cotton throughout.

2 The chart shows you each pattern and the angle at which it lies: fill in each petal shape by stitching right up to the outer edges of the outlines, but do not stitch over them.

3 To finish off, work a twelve point Algerian eyelet using one strand of black stranded cotton and one fine strand of gold metallic thread.

4 When the stitching is completed, carefully remove the tacking to produce the final 'patchworked' effect.

PETAL IN PATCHWORK KEY

DMC	ANCHOR	MADEIRA		COLOUR
Backstitch in one strand of stranded cotton				
310	403	Black		Black infill patterns
Eyelet stitch blending one strand of each thread				
310	403	Black		Black
DMC metallic No. 284				Gold centre

FINISHED SIZE: Stitch count 100 high x 97 wide
FABRIC AND APPROXIMATE FINISHED DESIGN AREA:
28HPI evenweave over two threads 7⅛x6⅞in
(18.1x17.5cm)

TIP

THIS TECHNIQUE CAN BE USED WITH ANY SHAPE. OUR BLACKWORK PATTERNS CREATE AN INTERESTING CONTRAST IN DENSITY AND TEXTURE: YOU COULD ADD VARIATION BY USING DIFFERENT WEIGHTS OF THREAD.

Centre point   Outside Tip

Photocopy to enlarge.
Chart shown at 65%

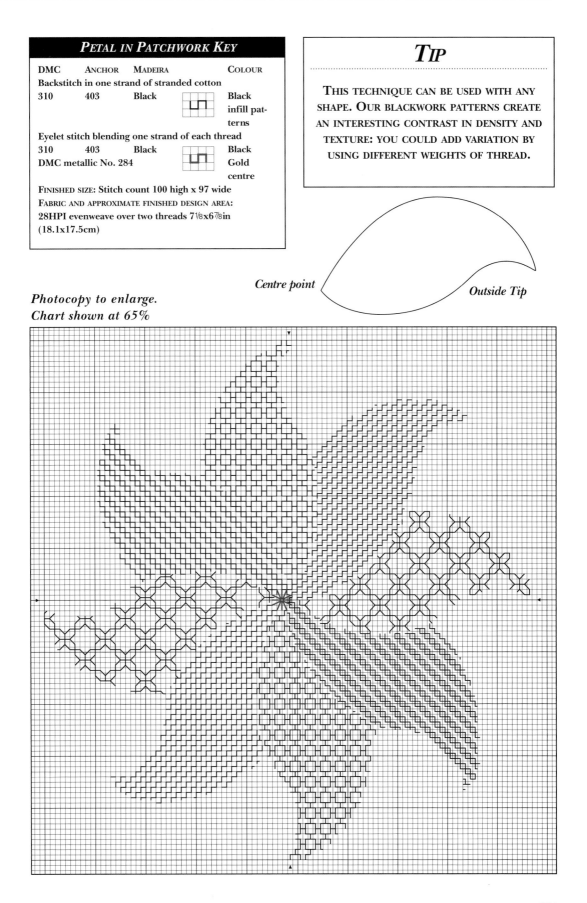

	B	C	B		
A	E	H	F	D
	I	L	K	
B				B
C	J	G	M	N	M	G	J	C
B				B
	K	L	I	
D	F	H	E	A
	B	C	B		

Specific stitching details:

A & D - The iris outlines are backstitched in one strand of black flower thread. The filling motifs are worked in one strand of black stranded cotton. Work the stems and leaves in one strand of black sewing thread.

B Stitch the outlines in one strand of black stranded cotton. The flower centres are stitched in black sewing thread.

C The butterfly outlines are alternately stitched in one or two strands of black stranded cotton. All details are stitched in one strand of black stranded cotton.

E & F - All outlines are stitched in two strands of black stranded cotton. All details are stitched in black sewing thread.

G, H, I & K - Backstitch all outlines and details in one strand of black stranded cotton. See the extra charted detail for the stitching order of Section G.

J Stitch the flower motifs in two strands of black stranded cotton. Using the same thread in two strands, then stitch the outer border lines around the flowers. Work the asterisks in the centre of the flowers in one strand of black stranded cotton. Finally stitch the fine line between the flower out-lines and the outer border in one strand of black sewing thread. The extra charted detail will show you the stitching order of this section.

L The patterns are alternately stitched in two strands of black stranded cotton or one strand of black sewing thread.

M Stitch the outlines in one strand of black stranded cotton. The centres are stitched in one strand of black sewing thread.

N **The Rose:**
1 Backstitch the outlines of the leaves, large and small, in two strands of black stranded cotton.
2 Backstitch the outlines of the rose and the stems in one strand of black flower thread.
3 Using one strand of black sewing thread, work the zig-zag pattern on the rose petals.
4 Work the detail on all leaves in one strand of black stranded cotton.
5 Having washed and pressed your work if necessary, mount it in the wooden tray

GENERAL HINTS

FOR ANYONE WHO FINDS WORKING WITH THE BLACK THREADS ON WHITE FABRIC DAZZLES THEIR EYES - WHY NOT CHOOSE CREAM OR ANY OTHER SOFTER SHADE OF FABRIC?

ALWAYS WORK WITH A SMALL PIECE OF STICKY TAPE OR MASKING TAPE TO HAND - AFTER UNPICKING, DAB THE MATERIAL WITH THE TAPE AND THIS WILL REMOVE ANY BLACK FLUFF LEFT BEHIND.

SITA WITH A LOTUS FLOWER

Behind this beautiful design lies a legendary tale from India.

The Story of Sita and Rama
The Diwali Festival is held in October and November and holds great significance in the Hindu and Sikh calendar. Hindus celebrate the time when the great king, Ram and his queen, Sita, returned to their kingdom after many adventures and battles against the forces of evil.

You Will Need

- **28 HPI evenweave - 12x9in(31x23cm), white (ref. NJ429.00)**
- **DMC stranded cotton - 310, black**
- **DMC Flower thread - 310, black**
- **DMC metallic thread - no.284, gold**
- **Polyester sewing thread - black**
- **Tapestry needle - size 26**
- **Frame - with 9x6½ in(23x16.5 cm) oval aperture, oval wood with gilt edge**
- **2 oz. wadding - 9x6½ in(23x16.5 cm) oval**

How to stitch the project

1 Most of the stitching is over two threads of evenweave; refer to the chart for accurate placing of all the outlines.

2 Backstitch the main outline and folds of the sari using two strands of black stranded cotton.

3 Using one strand of black flower thread, stitch the outlines and details of the lotus flowers.

4 With one whole strand of gold metallic thread, chain stitch around the border of the sari. When this is completed, backstitch the inner line of the sari border in one strand of embroidery cotton. (It is important that the inner line of the sari is worked after the gold chain.)

5 Stitch the hands, arms and facial details in one strand of stranded cotton. Use two or three straight stitches for the pupils of the eyes. Stitch the hair outline in one strand of black sewing thread.

6 Fill in the pattern on the sari in one strand of black sewing thread: the pattern is on a separate chart. Refer to the photograph as the pattern changes direction where the fabric is draped over Sita's head to give a feeling of movement. The vertical lines inside the sari fabric is stitched in one strand of black sewing cotton.

7 Now you can add the final details:
i) Long stitch the hair using three strands of black stranded cotton.
ii) For the earring, chain stitch two large loops in one whole strand of gold metallic thread.
iii) The long necklace is chain stitched in one whole strand of gold metallic thread. The shorter necklace (in a 'V' shape) is chain stitched in two fine strands of gold metallic thread.
iv) The bracelets on Sita's arm are backstitched in one whole strand of gold metallic thread.
v) The ring on her finger is stitched using one fine strand of gold metallic thread, backstitching several times over the same area.
vi) There is a double line of running stitch on the inside of the sari fabric, worked in one fine strand of gold metallic thread.

SITA KEY

DMC	ANCHOR	MADEIRA		COLOUR

Backstitch in two strands of stranded cotton

| 310 | 403 | Black | | Black outline and folds of sari |

Backstitch in one strand of stranded cotton

| 310 | 403 | Black | | Black inner line of sari, and arms, hands and face details |

Backstitch in one strand
DMC Flower
thread No. 2310 — Black lotus flowers

Backstitch in one strand
Polyester sewing cotton — Black hair outline, inside sari fabric, infill pattern (see instructions)

Backstitch in one whole strand
DMC metallic No. 284 — Gold bracelets

Backstitch in one fine strand
DMC metallic No. 284 — Gold ring and inside sleeve detail

Long stitch in three strands of stranded cotton

| 310 | 403 | Black | | Black hair |

Chain stitch in one whole strand
DMC metallic No. 284 — Gold border of sari, long necklace and earring

Chain stitch in two fine strands
DMC metallic No. 284 — Gold small necklace

FINISHED SIZE: Stitch count 95 high x 26 wide
FABRIC AND APPROXIMATE FINISHED DESIGN AREA:
28HPI evenweave over two threads 6¾x1⅞in
(17.1x4.8cm)

Infill patterns for Sita's sari

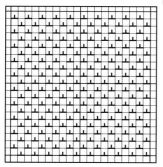

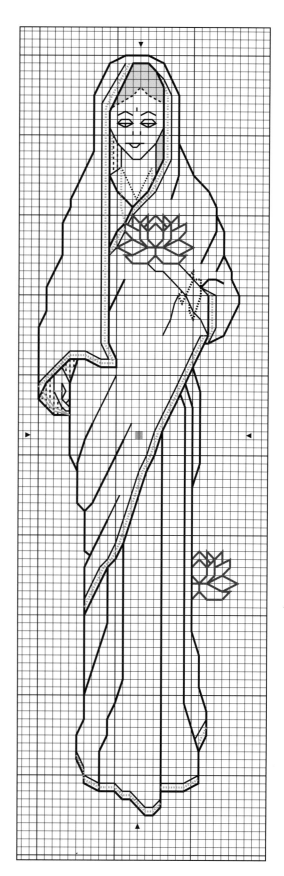

How to finish

1 With right sides together, stitch around the edges of the cushion cover (½in - 13mm seam allowance), leaving an 8in (20cm) gap along the fourth side unstitched. Trim the corners.

2 Turn the cover right side out, insert the cushion pad and slip stitch the edges of the opening neatly together with matching thread.

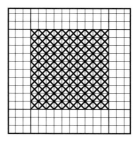

Leaf infill pattern

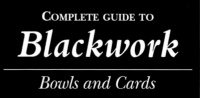

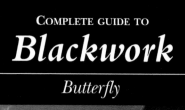

COMPLETE GUIDE TO
Blackwork
Butterfly

BUTTERFLY

An oriental design comprising symmetrical Blackwork patterns.

You Will Need

- 28 HPI evenweave - 10x10in(25x25cm), white
- DMC stranded cotton - 310, black
- DMC Stranded cotton - 310, black
- DMC Flower thread - 2310, black
- DMC Broder Spécial 16 - 310, black
- DMC Coton perlé 8 - 310, black
- DMC metallic thread - no.273, antique gold (optional)
- DMC metallic thread - no.284, gold
- Polyester sewing thread - black
- Tapestry needle - size 26
- Frame - 7½in square (19cm sq.)
- 2 oz. wadding

For the design

• A butterfly basking in the sun against the warmed brickwork is the subject for this blackwork project, which combines embroidery and metallic threads. Follow the instructions carefully for the velvet stitch which gives a wonderful texture to the butterfly's body.

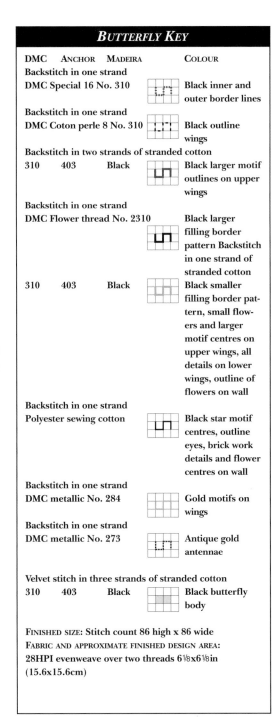

BUTTERFLY KEY

DMC	ANCHOR	MADEIRA		COLOUR
Backstitch in one strand				
DMC Special 16 No. 310				Black inner and outer border lines
Backstitch in one strand				
DMC Coton perle 8 No. 310				Black outline wings
Backstitch in two strands of stranded cotton				
310	403	Black		Black larger motif outlines on upper wings
Backstitch in one strand				
DMC Flower thread No. 2310				Black larger filling border pattern Backstitch in one strand of stranded cotton
310	403	Black		Black smaller filling border pattern, small flowers and larger motif centres on upper wings, all details on lower wings, outline of flowers on wall
Backstitch in one strand				
Polyester sewing cotton				Black star motif centres, outline eyes, brick work details and flower centres on wall
Backstitch in one strand				
DMC metallic No. 284				Gold motifs on wings
Backstitch in one strand				
DMC metallic No. 273				Antique gold antennae
Velvet stitch in three strands of stranded cotton				
310	403	Black		Black butterfly body

FINISHED SIZE: Stitch count 86 high x 86 wide
FABRIC AND APPROXIMATE FINISHED DESIGN AREA:
28HPI evenweave over two threads 6⅛x6⅛in
(15.6x15.6cm)

How to stitch

1 Work each stitch over two threads of the evenweave fabric. Having tacked the centre lines on your fabric as a guide, work the border as follows:

i) Stitch the inner and outer border lines in one strand of black Broder spécial 16.

ii) Work the larger filling pattern in one strand of black flower thread.

iii) The smaller pattern in stitched in one strand of black stranded cotton.

2 To act as a guide and to define the stitching area, outline the butterfly's body and wings in sewing thread.

3 Fill in the patterns on the wings: refer to the chart and key for details of positioning. The thickest outlines on the upper portion of the wings are stitched in two strands of black stranded cotton; the small flowers and the centre of the largest motifs are stitched in one strand of black stranded cotton; the centres of the star motifs are stitched in one strand of black sewing thread. On the lower section of the wings all black outlines and details are stitched in one strand of black stranded cotton. All gold details are stitched in one whole strand of gold metallic thread no. 284.

4 Backstitch the outline the wings in one strand of coton perlé no. 8.

5 Work the body of the butterfly in velvet stitch using three strands of black stranded cotton. The pile is trimmed quite close to the stitching to give a lovely fuzzy texture.

TIP

THIS AREA CAN BE WORKED IN SIMPLE CROSS STITCH IF PREFERRED.

---

6 Outline the eyes in one strand of black sewing thread.

TIP

BACKSTITCH THE ANTENNAE IN ONE WHOLE STRAND OF ANTIQUE GOLD METALLIC THREAD NO. 273. ONLY A 12INCH LENGTH OF THIS THREAD IS REQUIRED: IF YOU HAVEN'T GOT ANY, SUBSTITUTE ONE STRAND OF BLACK STRANDED COTTON.

---

7 Stitch the brickwork detailling on the wall in one strand of black sewing thread. The outlines of the flowers are stitched in one strand of black stranded cotton and the centres in one strand of black sewing thread.

Velvet stitch

Stitching over two threads, come up at 1 and down at 2, two threads to the right as in simple cross stitch.

Now come up again at 1 and down at 2 as if you were repeating the same stitch. Leave a loop for the 'pile' of the velvet by not pulling the thread right through the fabric.

Now come up at 3 and down at 4 to finish off the cross stitch, making sure that the loop is stitched down by this action. Work from the bottom of the stitching area, leaving one unstitched horizontal thread between the rows. The pile can be trimmed as in this case or left uncut.

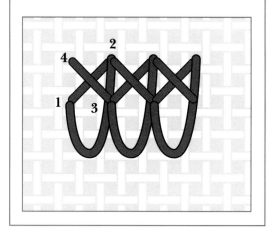

flames, decid...
publicly at th...
even as before...
which might...
opinion, product...
23rd of May the...
reconstructed before the...
reassembled, confident that...
deprived of a spectacle for wh...
yearned. Accordingly, toward elev...
Savonarola, Domenico Bonvicini, and S...
were brought to the place of execution; and...
degraded from their rank by the ecclesiastica...
were bound in the centre of an immense pile of...
all three to the same stake. Then the Bishop Pagna...
noli declared to the condemned that he separated them
forever... ...m the militant!"
re... ...arch trium-
...onarola, who from th... ...owing to his
...rdom, entered into the glories of... ...at that
...ant. This was all the victims uttered, ...arola,
moment an Arrabiato, a personal enemy of Sa...
breaking through the line formed by the guards o...
the scaffold, snatched a torch from the four corners of the p...
executioner, and set fire to the... his discip...
When the smoke arose, Savonarola and his
began to sing a psalm; and still, when wrapped in th...
devouring flames, the solemn strain was heard, which...
ascended to open for their souls an entrance through the...
gates of heaven.

L...
Ro...
each...
forwar...
followe...
dred lan...
and three...
raised fro...
August the...
men, which i...
of the Venetia...
to which it i...

COMPLETE GUIDE TO
Blackwork
Bookmark

BOOKMARK

A delicate keepsake for marking your place in a favourite tale.

You Will Need

- 🍃 **28 HPI jobelan - 10x6in(25x15cm), pale grey or white**
- 🍃 **DMC Stranded cotton - 310, black**
- 🍃 **DMC Flower thread - 2310, black**
- 🍃 **DMC metallic thread - no.273, gold**
- 🍃 **DMC Broder spécial 16 - 310, black**
- 🍃 **Polyester sewing threads - black, white**
- 🍃 **Tapestry needle - size 26**
- 🍃 **2mm black ribbon - 5in (13cm) length**
- 🍃 **White felt for backing - 2x8in (5x20cm)**
- 🍃 **Stiff cardboard (for the tassel)**

How to stitch the Bookmark

1 The stitches are worked over two threads The rows are marked A - H, starting from the top of the bookmark.

2 The outer borders are stitched as follows: the inner edge is stitched in one strand of black Flower thread; the middle line is stitched in one strand of stranded cotton and the outer edge in one strand of black Broder spécial.

3 The Star motif at the top and bottom of the bookmark: the main outline is stitched in black flower thread with details in metallic thread. Backstitch the next line in one strand of metallic thread.

Row A: The squares are stitched alternately in broder spécial 16 and flower thread. The fine detail is added using black sewing thread. Chain stitch the next line in one strand of metallic thread.

Row B: The heavy design is stitched in two strands of stranded cotton and the remainder in one strand of stranded cotton. Backstitch the next line in one strand of Broder Spécial 16.

Row C: Stitch this row using two strands of stranded cotton or a single strand of sewing thread where indicated. Backstitch the next line in one strand of metallic thread.

Row D: The butterfly motif is stitched in one strand of flower thread. Chain stitch the next line in one strand of metallic thread.

Row E: The larger motifs are stitched in one strand of flower thread and all the small crosses in one strand of sewing thread. Backstitch the next line in one strand of metallic thread.

Row F: Work the heavy outlines in one strand of flower thread and the central motif in one strand of sewing thread. Backstitch next line in one strand of Broder Spécial 16.

Row G: The fine honeycomb motif is stitched in one strand of stranded cotton; the heavier motifs are worked in two strands of stranded cotton. Chain stitch the next line in one strand of metallic thread.

Row H: The zig-zag is stitched in either flower thread or Broder Spécial 16 where indicated. Backstitch the next line in one strand of metallic thread.

How to finish

1 Cut around the outer edge of the bookmark, leaving a ½in (13mm) margin.

2 Fold all raw edges underneath, making neat points at either end first and then turning the side edges under. Lightly press and tack them into place. Make tassel, following instructions overleaf.

4 Insert the thread (with tassel attached) into the fold made by the point at the base of the bookmark and stitch into place.

5 Fold the ribbon in half and stitch into place at the tip of the bookmark.

6 Cut out the backing felt to just less than the size of the bookmark and slip stitch neatly into place.

BOOKMARK KEY

DMC	ANCHOR	MADEIRA	COLOUR

Backstitch in one strand

DMC Special 16 No. 310 — Black outer edge of border, pattern breaks, rows A, H

Backstitch in two strands of stranded cotton

| 310 | 403 | Black | Black rows B, C, G |

Backstitch in one strand

DMC Flower thread No. 2310 — Black inner edge of border, star motifs, rows A, D, E, F, H

Backstitch in one strand of stranded cotton

| 310 | 403 | Black | Black middle line of border, row B, G |

Backstitch in one strand of metallic thread

DMC metallic No. 273 — Antique gold pattern breaks, star motifs

Backstitch in one strand

Polyester sewing cotton — Black rows A, C, E, F

Chain stitch in one strand of metallic thread

DMC metallic No. 273 — Antique gold pattern breaks

FINISHED SIZE: Stitch count 93 high x 22 wide

FABRIC AND APPROXIMATE FINISHED DESIGN AREA:
28HPI jobelan over two threads 6⅝x1½in (16.8x3.8cm)

How to make a Tassel

1 Wind sufficient thread around the card for the tassel. If you wish, you can incorporate a length of metallic thread.

2 Hold tightly to the top of the bunch of wound threads and cut through them at the base of the card.

3 Fold a 9in (23cm) piece of thread in half; slip the looped end under the cut threads and take it up to the top of the tassel. Pass the ends of the folded thread through the loop and tighten.

4 Now bind the strands by cutting another piece of thread. Double it and place the looped end against the tassel. Wind the thread firmly around the tassel.

5 To finish, slip the ends through the loop. Pull tightly on both ends and the loop will be drawn into the centre of the binding. Neaten the ends.

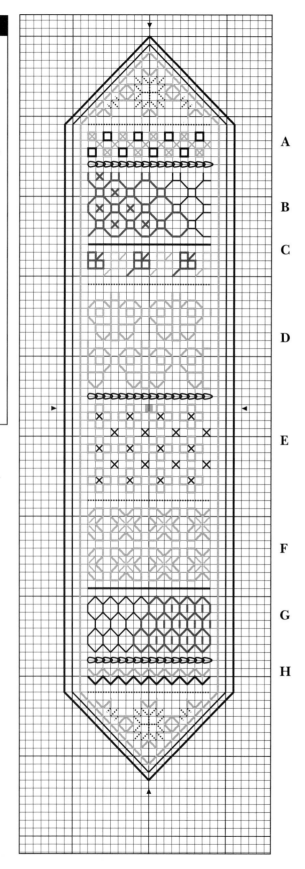

DESK SET AND LETTER RACK

A co-ordinating pattern darning design to enhance any desktop.

This matching pair of designs incorporate pattern darning to give a more masculine feel, which is quite appropriate in this setting. The addition of a colour other than black makes a interesting contrast. Pattern darning is achieved quite simply by working blocks and lines of running stitch to create a geometric effect on the fabric. If you would like to know more about this technique, read pages 13 for more information.

You Will Need for the Desk Set

- 30 HPI evenweave - 6x6in(15x15cm), pale blue (ref. NJ737.11)
- DMC stranded cotton - 310, 517
- DMC Broder Spécial 16 - 310, black
- DMC metallic thread - no.274, antique silver
- Tapestry needle - size 26
- 2oz. wadding - 3x3in (7.5x7.5cm)
- Wood Desk Kit - ref WDK (from Framecraft Miniatures)

You Will Need for the Letter Rack

- 30 HPI evenweave - 10x8in(25x20cm), pale blue (ref. NJ737.11)
- DMC stranded cotton - 310, 517
- DMC Broder Spécial 16 - 310, black
- DMC metallic thread - no.274, antique silver
- Tapestry needle - size 26
- 2oz. wadding - 4¾x2¼in (12x5.5cm)
- Letter Rack (from Canopia tel. 01895 235005)

How to stitch the projects

1 Use one strand of black DMC Broder Spécial 16 in both projects to stitch the centre pattern blocks.

2 The black stranded cotton is used in one strand to stitch the inner border lines in running stitch and three strands for the outer black border patterning.

3 The blue stranded cotton is also used in three strands in the centre of the design.

4 The corner motifs are stitched in two strands of DMC metallic thread no. 274.

5 The projects are mounted in the items according to the manufacturer's instructions.

TIPS

TAKE CARE IF YOU NEED TO PRESS YOUR FABRIC BEFORE MOUNTING - SET YOUR IRON TO A COOL SETTING AS THE METALLIC THREAD MAY MELT AT HIGH TEMPERATURES.

THE DESK SET TOP DESIGN WILL FIT INTO ANY OF FRAMECRAFT'S 2⅝IN ROUND CHINA BOX LIDS.

WHY NOT CHANGE THE COLOURS OF THREAD AND FABRIC TO MATCH YOUR OFFICE DÉCOR? MAKE SURE THAT THE CONTRAST BETWEEN FABRIC AND THREAD IS STRONG ENOUGH TO SHOW.

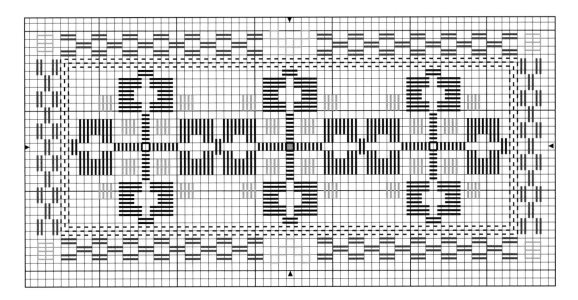

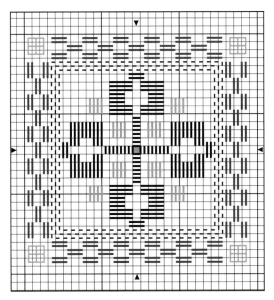

PEN HOLDER AND LETTER RACK KEY

DMC	ANCHOR	MADEIRA		COLOUR

Backstitch in one strand
DMC Special 16 No. 310 — Black centre

Backstitch in three strands of stranded cotton

310	403	Black		Black border
517	169	1107		Blue centre

Backstitch in one strand of stranded cotton

310	403	Black		Black inner border

Backstitch in two strands
DMC metallic No. 274 — Antique silver corners and centre border motif on letter rack

Our model was stitched using DMC threads; the Anchor and Madeira conversions are not necessarily exact colour equivalents.

FINISHED SIZE OF PEN HOLDER: Stitch count
28 high x 28 wide
FABRIC AND APPROXIMATE FINISHED DESIGN AREA:
30HPI evenweave over two threads
1⅞x1⅞in (4.8x4.8cm)
Finished size of letter rack: Stitch count
28 high x 65 wide
Fabric and approximate finished design area:
30HPI evenweave over two threads 1⅞x4⅜in
(4.8x11.1cm)

STUART LADY

Blackwork designs create a most becoming period costume.

For the Project

You Will Need

- 28 HPI evenweave - 12x9in(31x23cm), white (ref. NJ429.00)
- DMC stranded cotton - 310, black
- Balger braid - fine #8, gold
- Madeira metallic thread - no.34, gold
- Polyester sewing thread - black and white
- Seed beads - four, pearl white
- Scrap of fine net or chiffon - 2in (5cm) for neckline, black
- 2mm wide fine ribbon - 3in (7.5cm), black
- Tapestry needle - size 24 and 26
- Beading needle
- Large-eyed sewing needle
- Frame - with 9x6½ in(23x16.5 cm) oval aperture, oval wood with gilt edge
- 2 oz. wadding - 9x6½ in(23x16.5 cm) oval

STUART LADY KEY

DMC	ANCHOR	MADEIRA		COLOUR
BACKSTITCH IN TWO STRANDS				
310	403	Black		Black outline bodice and top of underskirt, lace holes, four bands at base and folds of under-skirt
BACKSTITCH IN ONE STRAND				
310	403	Black		Black outline and folds of fan; outline and details of face, neck and arms
BACKSTITCH IN ONE STRAND				
Polyester sewing cotton				Black chemise cuff, inside of overskirt
BACKSTITCH IN ONE STRAND				
Balger Fine Braid No. 8				Gold outline and folds of overskirt, two outer lines on front panel of underskirt
LONG STITCH IN ONE STRAND				
Balger Fine Braid No. 8				Gold fan edging
BACKSTITCH IN TWO FINE STRANDS				
Madeira Gold No. 34				Gold top edge and details on fan, centre line on front panel of under skirt
BACKSTITCH IN ONE FINE STRAND				
Madeira Gold No. 34				Gold pattern on over-skirt, couching of net neck line
APPLY PEARL BEADS				
with one strand				Pearl white sewing cotton necklace
FRENCH KNOTS IN TWO STRANDS				
310	403	Black		Black hair detail
LONG STITCH IN SIX STRANDS				
310	403	Black		Black hair and ringlets
APPLY BLACK NET				
with two strands Madeira Gold No. 34				Black net neckline
APPLY BLACK RIBBON				
with one strand				Black black sewing cotton ribbon waistband

FINISHED SIZE: Stitch count 104 high x 49 wide
FABRIC AND APPROXIMATE FINISHED DESIGN AREA:
28HPI Quaker cloth over two threads 7⅜x3½in (18.7x8.9cm)

How to Stitch the Outlines

1 Most of the stitching is over two threads of evenweave; refer to the chart for accurate placing of all stitching lines.

2 Use a size 26 tapestry needle for the stranded cotton and the sewing cotton. Use the size 24 needle when stitching with gold thread. The larger eye prevents the thread from stripping.

3 Work the outlines and detail of the bodice, sleeve, top part of the overskirt; the underskirt and folds and the four lines at the base of the underskirt using two strands of black stranded cotton.

4 The outlines and details of the face, neck hands, arms and fan are worked in one strand of black stranded cotton. For the pupils of the eyes stitch three straight stitches closely together as shown on the chart.

5 Work the sleeve cuff in one strand of black sewing thread.

6 Use two strands of Madeira Gold No. 34 thread for the top edge and detail on the fan and the centre of the front panel of the underskirt.

7 Work the outlines of the folds on the overskirt, the two outer lines on the front panel of the underskirt and the front edge of the fan.

8 Now you can add the blackwork pattern details:

i) Fill in the bodice and sleeve areas with blackwork pattern 1 using one strand of black stranded cotton.
ii) The overskirt is partly worked with the same pattern, this time using one strand of Madeira Gold No. 34.
iii) The underskirt is filled with pattern 2. The small crosses and points of the large cross are worked in one strand of black stranded cotton; the large cross is worked in one strand of black sewing thread.

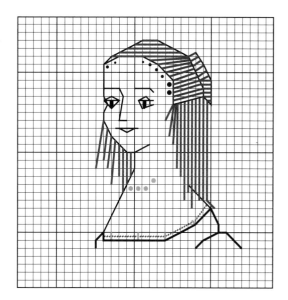

The Head Detail

Pattern 1

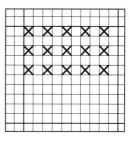 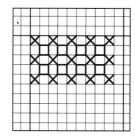

Pattern 2

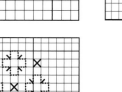

69

How to Stitch the Head Detail

1 The enlarged chart will help you place the stitches accurately on the head to achieve the hair detail. The hair is worked in two sections; the top part (A) and the ringlets (B).

2 Section A is worked in long stitch using six strands of stranded cotton. The direction of the stitches is shown on the chart.

3 Section B is also worked in black stranded cotton. First work vertical long stitches as shown on the chart using six strands; then place small horizontal stitches down the length of each long stitch to give the texture and appearance of ringlets.

4 Work the small curls on the forehead as French knots using two strands of black stranded cotton. Vary the size of the knots by varying the number of twists of the needle around the thread.

5 Attach the beads around the neck at the points shown on the chart using the white sewing thread and the beading needle.

How to Work the Neckline

1 Cut a small strip of fine black net about ¼in (6mm) wide and 2in (5cm) in length. Thread this strip through a large-eyed needle and bring it up through the fabric at the left edge if the neckline.

2 Couch the net down at 5mm intervals along the neckline using one strand of Madeira Gold No. 34, with small vertical stitches.

3 When you have couched the net down from left to right along the neckline, take the net through to the back of the fabric and attach both ends to the back of the fabric using black sewing thread.

How to Attach the Ribbon at the Waistband

1 Thread the ribbon through a large-eyed needle and bring it up through the fabric at one edge of the bodice along the waistband line. Take it back down at the other end of the line.

2 Fasten the ribbon to the bodice with small stab stitches in one strand of black sewing thread. Secure the ribbon ends at the back of the fabric with small stitches in black sewing thread.

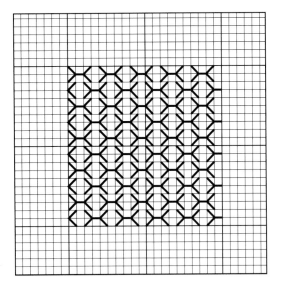

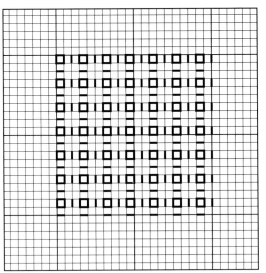

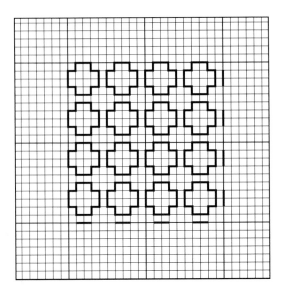

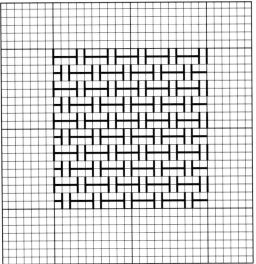

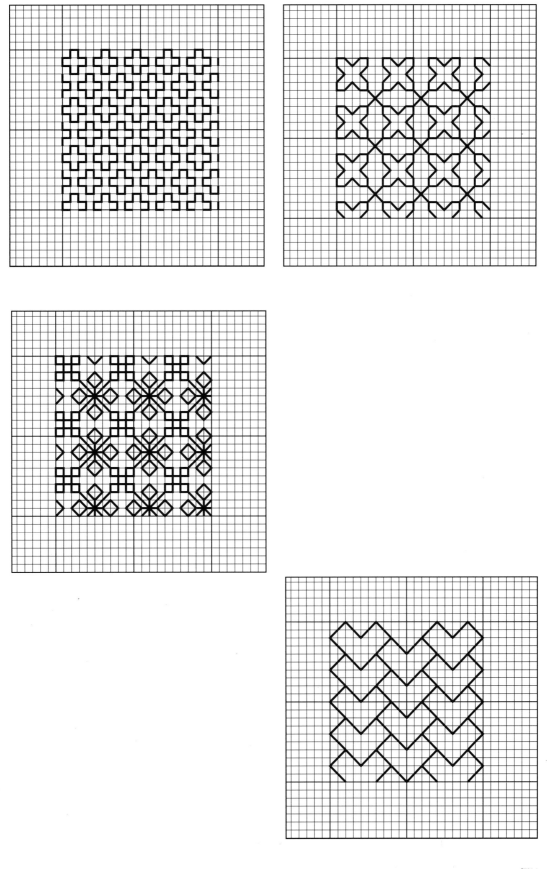

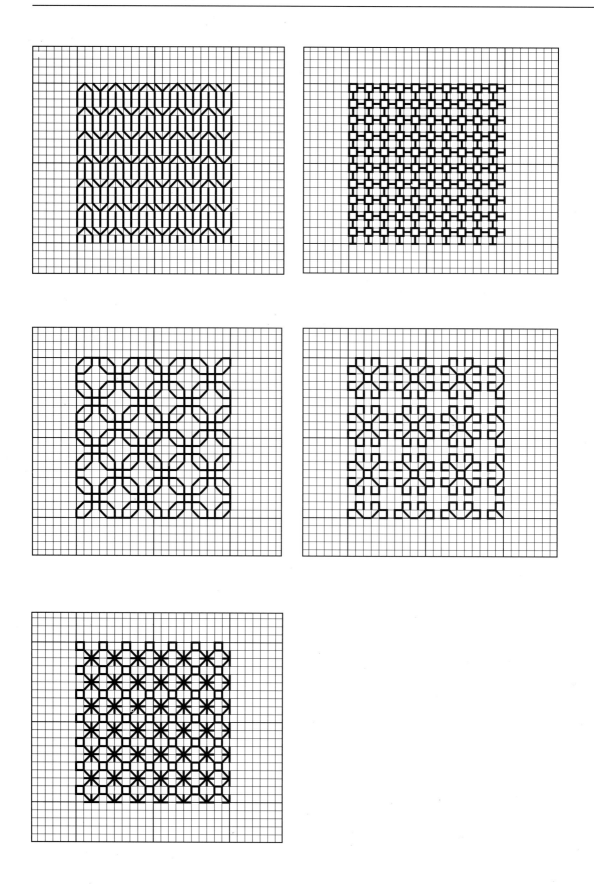

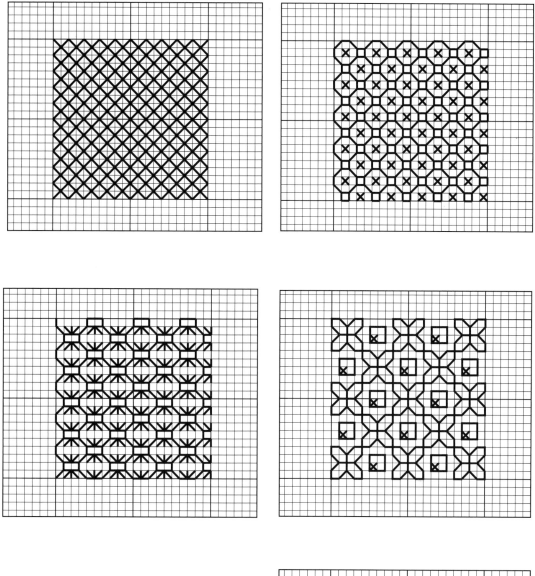

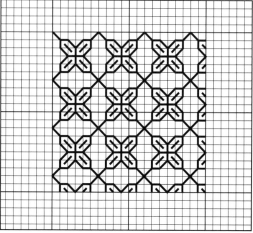

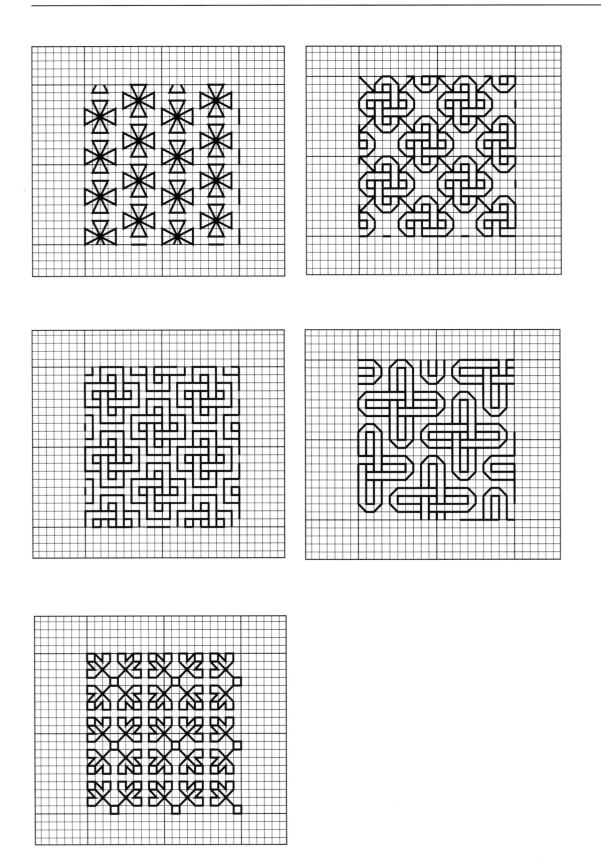

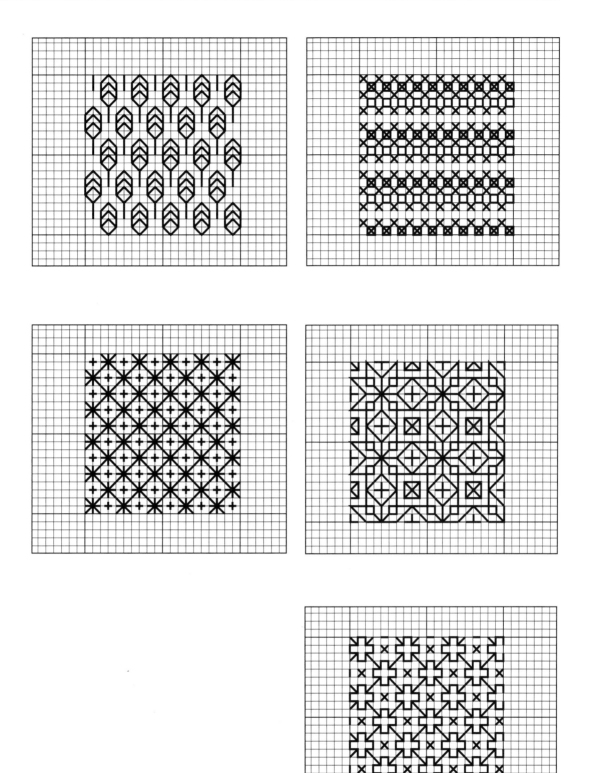

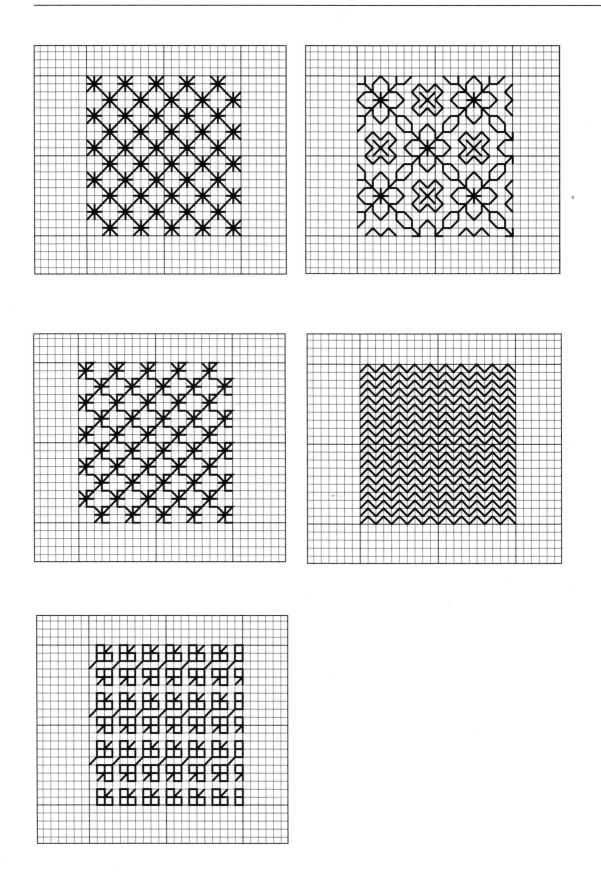

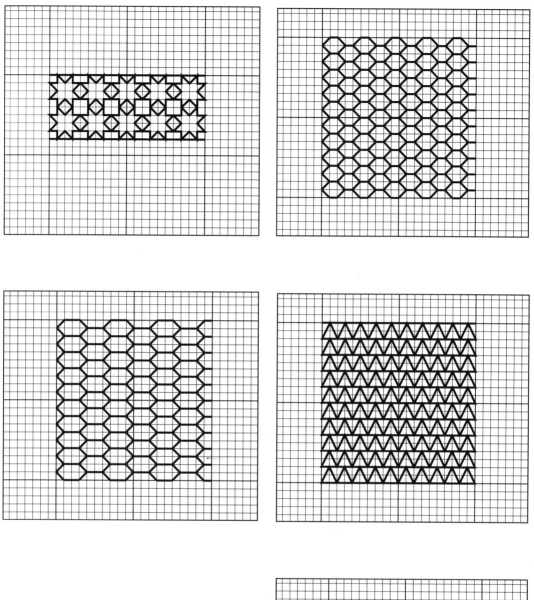

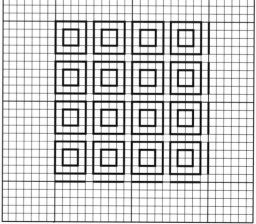

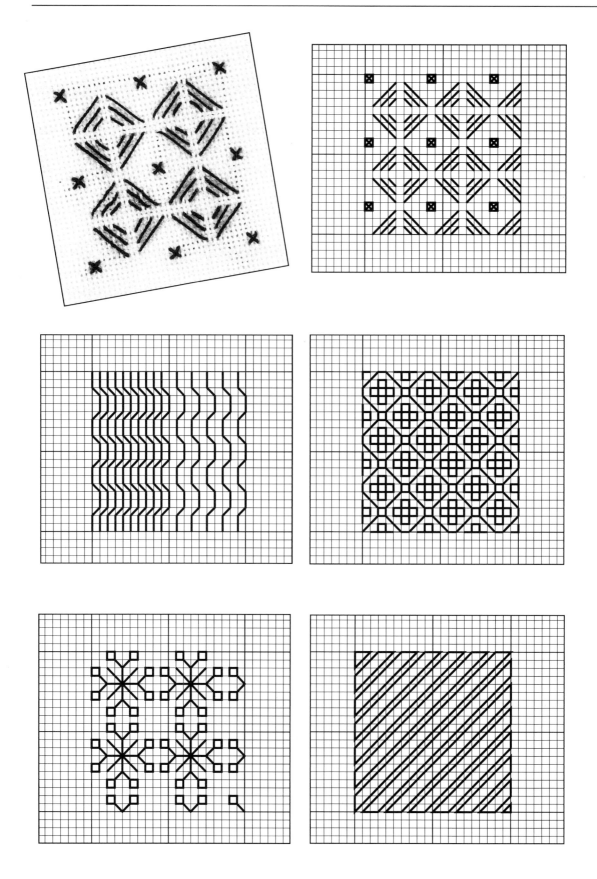

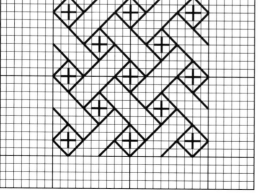

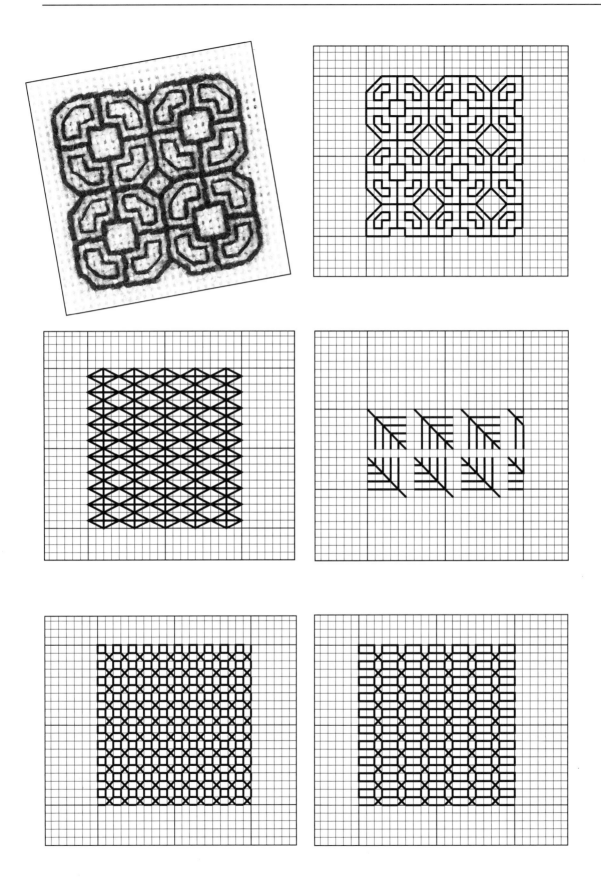

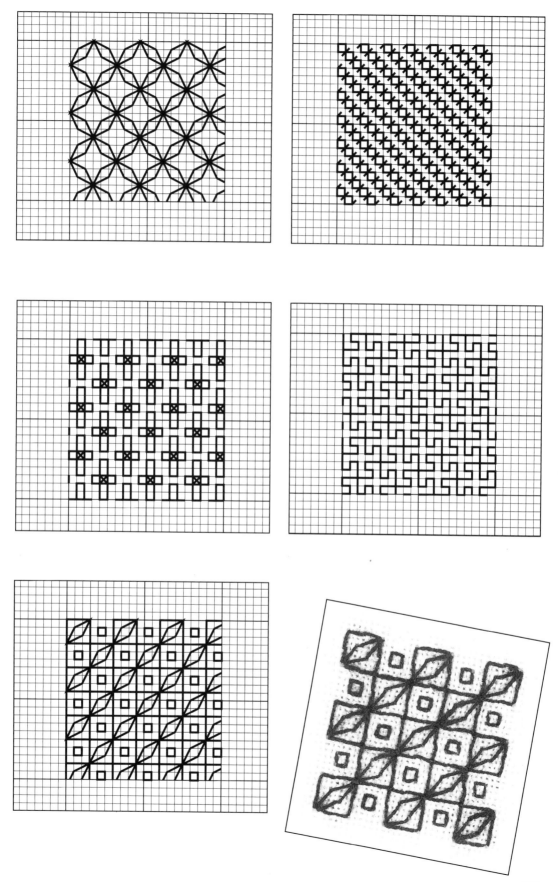

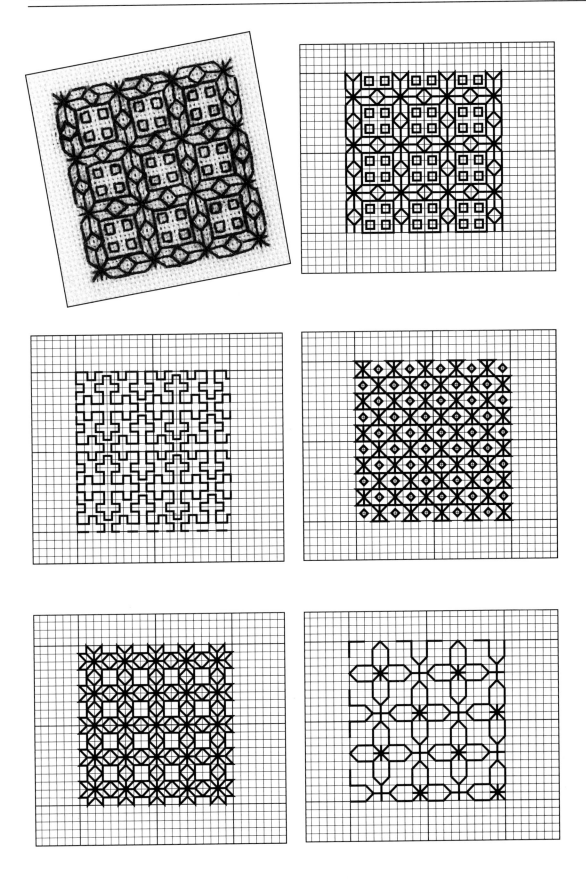

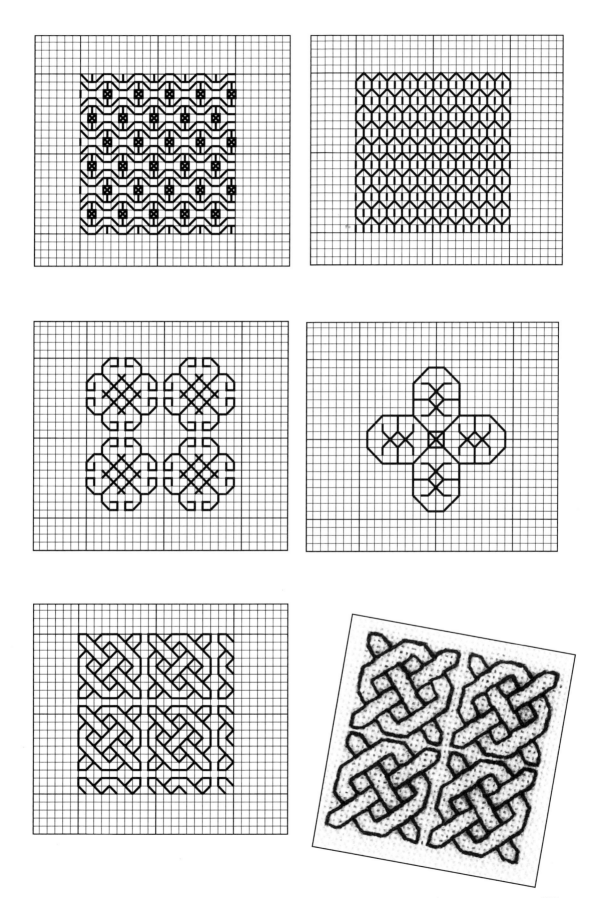

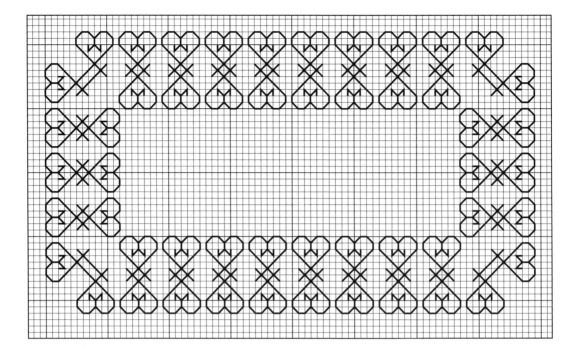

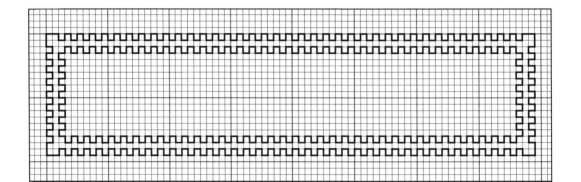

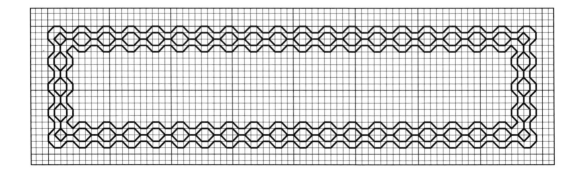

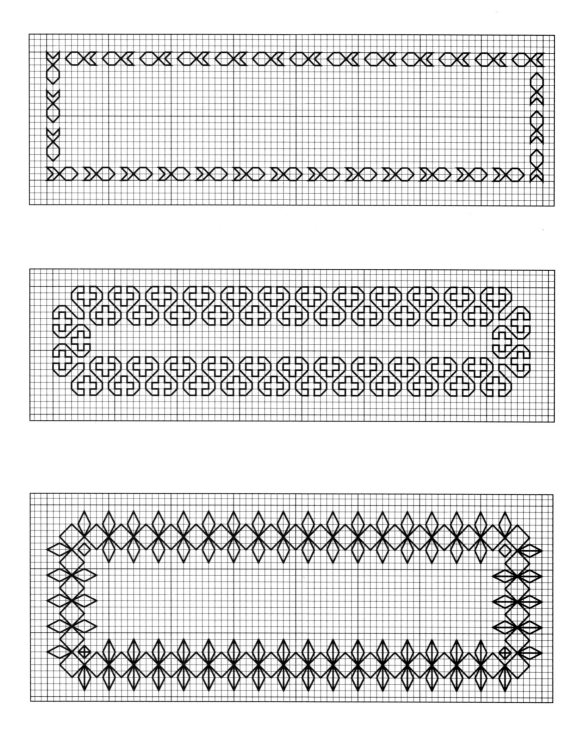

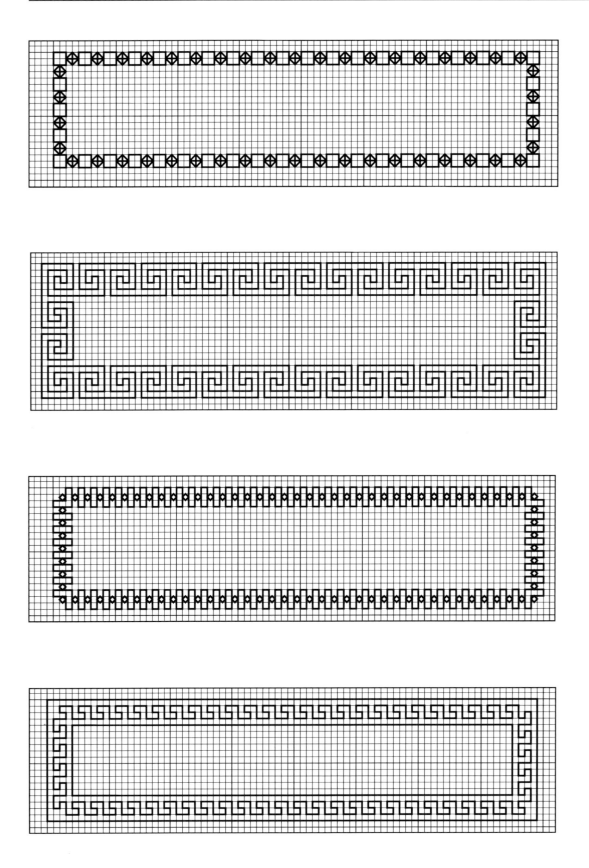

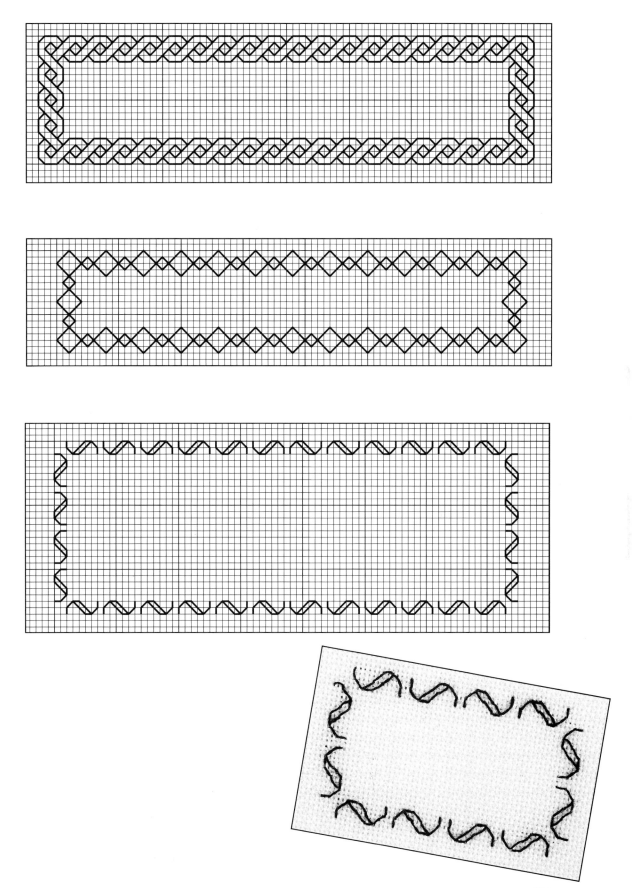

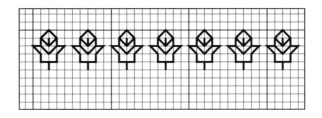

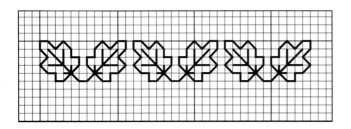

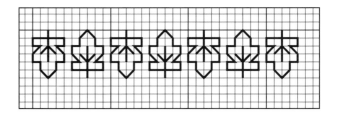

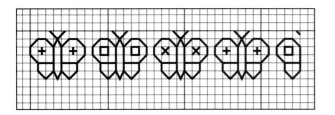

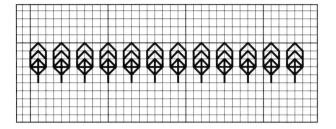

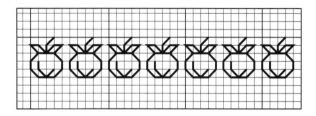

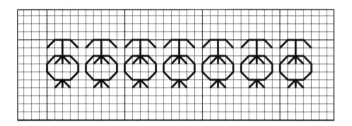

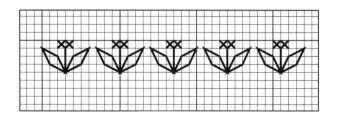

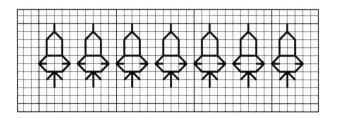

Appendices

Suppliers:
• **FABRIC** supplied by Fabric Flair Limited,
The Old Brewery, The Close,
Warminster,Wiltshire, BA12 9AL
Tel: (01985) 214466

• **THREADS** supplied by DMC - for details of
nearest stockist, please contact:
DMC Creative World, Pullman Road,
Wigston, Leicestershire, LE18 2DY
Tel:(01533) 811040

• Crystal and porcelain bowls, address book,
desk set, wooden tray from Framecraft
Miniatures Ltd. Tel: (0121) 212 0551
• Letter Rack from Canopia (01895) 235005
• Towel with aida band from Wimble Bees
Tel:(01235) 771731

Bibliography

• The Oxford Reference Dictionary: Oxford
University Press ISBN 0 19 863143 X
• Blackwork Embroidery by Margaret
Pascoe: Batsford Books 1986
• Blackwork Embroidery by Elizabeth
Geddes and Moyra McNeill: Dover
Publications 0 486 23245-X
• Seasons of Splendour by Madhur Jaffrey:
Puffin ISBN 0-14-034699-6
• Cross Stitch Calligraphy by Iva Polansky:
Kyle Cathie Ltd
ISBN 1 85626 089 5

Galleries and other sources of information:
•Victoria & Albert Museum, London
• National Portrait Gallery, London
• The Royal School of Needlework,
Apartment 12A, Hampton Court Palace,
East Moseley, Surrey KT8 9AU
Tel: (0181) 943 1432

Acknowledgements

With special thanks to my family and friends
for their interest and support; to Rebecca
Bradshaw for her encouragement; Kate John
for her patience; Cara Ackerman for her
advice; Karen Reed for her charting exper-
tise and devotion to duty and last but not
least, to Barbara Phillips whose creative gift
has surpassed all my expectations.

Buy Needlecraft today

nd discover new projects, techniques and worthwhile stitching advice!

Our four-weekly magazine offers you a wealth of wonderful projects, genuine guidance and practical advice on a host of stitching disciplines ✦

Needlecraft magazine combines all types of needlecraft, old and new and is an ideal guide for beginners and experienced stitchers alike ✦ You'll find it easy to learn patchwork and quilting, improve your cross stitching or produce a stunning needlepoint picture with Needlecraft ✦

Experts, like Jane Greenoff, give advice on how to work on new projects offering you their hard earned experience. Helping you complete a design with the minimum fuss and effort ✦

You'll find Needlecraft available in all good newsagents and in some supermarkets and specialist stitching shops ✦ It's an ideal source of first-rate advice and new designs from popular designers ✦ Go out and treat yourself ✦

On sale now only £2.75

✦ TO SUBSCRIBE JUST CALL – 01225 822511 ✦

THIS IS THE PROPERTY OF
SOUTH WORCESTERSHIRE COLLEGE
SCHOOL OF ARTS

[illegible library stamp]

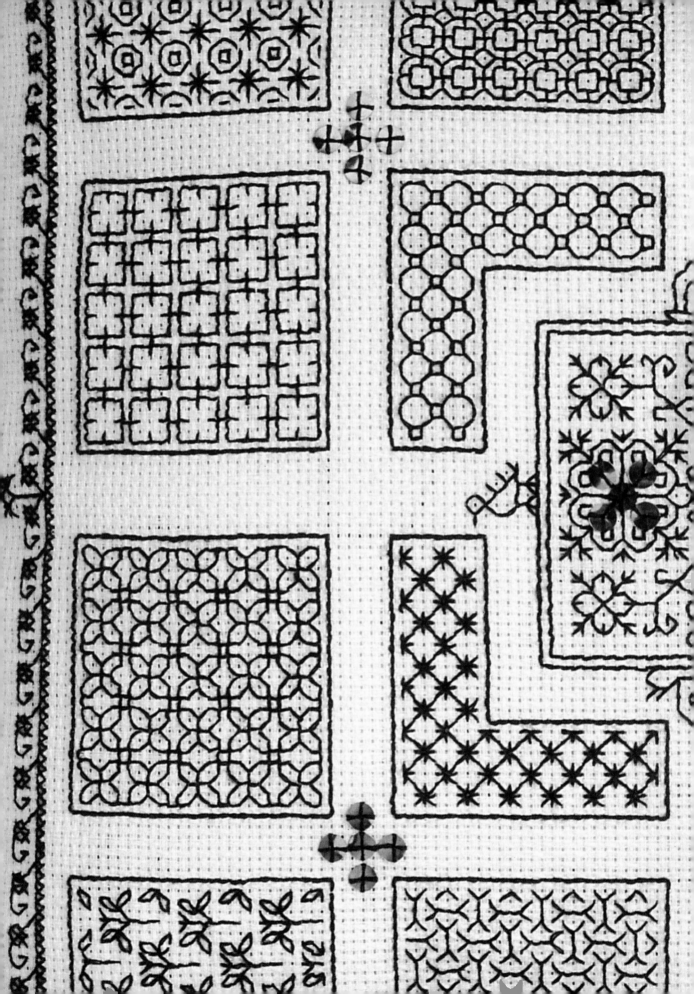